Write On!

SUPER STORYTELLING

Written by Charis Mather

KidHaven PUBLISHING

Published in 2026 by
KidHaven Publishing, an Imprint of
Greenhaven Publishing, LLC
2544 Clinton St., Buffalo, NY 14224

Written by: Charis Mather
Edited by: Rebecca Phillips-Bartlett
Designed by: Jasmine Pointer

Cataloging-in-Publication Data
Names: Mather, Charis.
Title: Super storytelling/ Charis Mather.
Description: Bufalo, New York : Kidhaven Publishing, 2026. | Series: Write On! | Includes glossary and index
Identifiers: ISBN 9781534550452 (pbk) | ISBN 9781534550469 (library bound) | ISBN 9781534550476 (ebook)
Subjects: LCSH: Authorship—Juvenile Literature | Creative writing—Juvenile Literature Classification: LCC PN159 M38 2026 | DDC 808.02-dc25

Manufactured in the United States of America

CPSIA compliance information: Batch #CSKH26
For further information contact Greenhaven Publishing LLC at 1-844-317-7404.

Please visit our website, www.greenhavenpublishing.com.
For a free color catalog of all our high-quality books, call toll free 1-844-317-7404 or fax 1-844-317-7405.

Find us on

Image Credits

All images are courtesy of Shutterstock.com, unless otherwise stated.

Cover – Monkey Business Images, SpicyTruffel, NotionPic, VectorHot. Throughout – SpicyTruffel, NotionPic. 4–5 – Prostock-studio, Luis Louro. 6–7 – Dmytro Zinkevych, ESB Professional. 8–9 – Pixel-Shot, T.TATSU. 10–11 – Krotnakro, Corona Borealis Studio, Tunatura, PeopleImages.com - Yuri A. 12–13 – New Africa, Jens Ottoson, Skolova. 14–15 – Roman Samborskyi, CreativeAngela, Denis---S, Konmac, Paustowski, KajzrPhotography, PeopleImages.com - Yuri A. 16–17 – Supie Davis, red mango. 18–19 – PeopleImages.com - Yuri A. 20–21 – Artsiom P, Kabachki.photo. 22–23 – VH-studio, wavebreakmedia.

CONTENTS

Words that look like <u>this</u> can be found in the glossary on page 24.

YOU CAN WRITE

Is your mind full of stories, like mine is? Do you wish you could write them down for people to read? Guess what? You can! Anyone can write a story—they just have to learn how.

I am Professor Hoot. My job is to teach extraordinary kids how to become extraordinary writers. With a little patience and a lot of pencils, I can help you turn your ideas into super stories.

WHAT'S SO SUPER ABOUT STORYTELLING?

Stories are great for getting your imagination going. When I was a little owl, my parents read me lots of stories. Their stories gave me ideas for my own stories. I have been writing ever since.

Stories are also a great way to learn. Lessons are easier to remember when you have an example from a story. Stories can make learning much more interesting too.

WHY DO STORYTELLING SKILLS MATTER?

It is possible to make interesting stories seem uninteresting by telling them poorly. Good storytellers make stories simple enough to understand but detailed enough to be exciting.

Storytellers also have to pace their stories properly. It is a little like how athletes pace themselves when they run. Stories that drag out too long or end too suddenly can be boring or confusing.

SETTING UP YOUR STORY

Stories do not start on paper—they start in your brain! Before you start writing, you need to have an idea of the who, where, and what of your story.

Who?

Every story needs characters with different goals.

Where?

The locations stories take place at are called settings. Settings include where and when stories happen.

What?

The things that happen in your story make up the plot. A plot has a beginning, middle, and end.

PLANNING THE PERFECT PLOT

The Beginning

The beginning of your story should introduce your main characters and settings. This is where your readers get to know what kind of story they are about to read.

The beginning of a story is your chance to grab a reader's interest. Once they learn who the story is about and where it takes place, they should wonder what happens next.

The Middle

The middle of a story is where the main events happen. At this point, characters usually run into problems that get in the way of their goals. Then, characters start trying to solve their problems.

THE PROBLEM IN A STORY IS KNOWN AS THE CONFLICT.

You can add in some surprising twists and turns during the middle of your story. Just make sure they lead to an ending that makes sense.

YOU CAN BRING IN NEW CHARACTERS AND SETTINGS TOO. MAYBE YOU COULD INCLUDE A TALKING OWL!

The End

The end is where we find out how the problems from the middle of the story have been dealt with. Some problems might have been solved. Others might not have been.

If a lot has changed since the beginning of the story, the writer can show that at the end.

Some endings set up new problems. These kinds of endings are called cliffhangers.

A LESSON TO LEARN

Many stories contain a moral. A moral is a lesson, especially one that teaches you how to treat other people well.

A good way to include morals in your stories is to show characters learning those lessons. If your characters realize that they should change how they treat others, your readers might realize that too.

STORY-SHOW-ING, NOT STORY-TELL-ING

One of the most important skills a storyteller can have is not actually telling—it is showing! Showing is about helping readers imagine something using the senses, instead of just telling them about it.

Showing is especially helpful when you are describing characters. Take a look at these examples. Which sentence helps you imagine the girl more clearly?

Telling

She was sad.

Showing

She sniffled and wiped the tears from her eyes.

READ ON, WRITE ON

Aren't stories just su-hoo-per? The more you practice your storytelling, the easier it will become to share the wonderful stories in your imagination with others.

IS WRITING STORIES DIFFICULT? DON'T GIVE UP! LEARNING NEW SKILLS TAKES TIME.

Try reading stories that other people have written to give yourself ideas. You can learn a lot by asking questions about their characters, settings, and plots. So read on, write on, and enjoy!

GLOSSARY

goals	things that people want and work toward
locations	the places where things happen
pace	to keep at the right speed
senses	the ways we take in information from the world around us through sight, hearing, smell, taste, and touch

INDEX